Spiritual Development through Astrology

Spiritual Development through Astrology

41 Steps to Guide Your Way

Lynne Conant

iUniverse, Inc.
Bloomington

Spiritual Development through Astrology
41 Steps to Guide Your Way

iUniverse books may be ordered through booksellers or by contacting:

iUniverse
1663 Liberty Drive
Bloomington, IN 47403
www.iuniverse.com
1-800-Authors (1-800-288-4677)

ISBN: 978-1-4759-4453-2 (sc)
ISBN: 978-1-4759-4454-9 (ebk)

Library of Congress Control Number: 2012914604

Printed in the United States of America

iUniverse rev. date: 08/28/2012

Contents

Acknowledgments

Zoltan Mason was a fine astrologer and teacher of the art and science of astrology. Because of his knowledge and teaching, I was inspired to write this book.

His wife, Edith Mason, has also been a wonderful friend who through our many years of friendship helped me stay focused on what was really important.

I greatly appreciate the patience of my daughter, Kim, who has, in large part, made this journey with me.

Thanks to my friends and family who have always brought out the best in me.

Introduction

You may have personal reasons and circumstances that take you off the beaten path of life and into a more introspective state of mind. Maybe it's because you've had an experience that has you searching for a way to integrate this new experience into your life, or you are looking to put things into perspective. Whatever the catalyst, you are on a new path of discovery.

It was my study of astrology that breathed new life into an old one. It transformed an ordinary life into an extraordinary one. Through the study of astrology I learned many things about myself, and this led to a far more interesting journey than I could have imagined. It led me to better understand the inner workings of the soul and how it is gradually realized by the spirit. It is a journey that continues today, but with a much lighter heart.

The study of the astrological archetype is the most interesting. It answers all the questions of human interaction. The archetype begins with the sign Aries and moves counterclockwise toward Taurus, Gemini, moving through each sign to the last, Pisces. The nature of the signs speaks volumes about our lives and purposes. By understanding the nature of the signs, the planets that rule them, and the way planets act in each sign, we gain the knowledge of practical living.

Spiritual development can be ascertained in the same way by studying the archetype beginning with Pisces and moving in a clockwise direction toward Aquarius, Capricorn, and moving through each sign to the last, Aries.

Astrology is a soft science based on observation. Planets influence us the way that we receive the planetary influences. Planets influence us through position, disposition, aspect, and ricochet. The material in *Spiritual Development through Astrology* was derived through synthesizing these influences.

In the end, the practical and spiritual become one. No one can teach spiritual evolution. It is a journey that we must take on our own. We must find our own way.

Whether we believe in God in the Judeo-Christian sense of the word, higher influences, the laws of nature, or any other religious belief system, most have common ground. Through this interpretation I have tried to find the values that are shared by all human beings.

Spiritual Development through Astrology is an interpretation of the archetype and is written to give the reader encouragement in this solitary journey. You may read any passage at random. You can read it from the beginning to the end or from the end to the beginning.

House 1: Pisces

Feminine, Mutable, Water

1. Spiritual Evolution

Spiritual evolution is a process through which the soul of man, the unconscious, is realized by the spirit, the conscious.

The spirit is evolved. The soul is unevolved, instinctual, and animalistic. It is the soul that evolves to realize the brilliance of the divine spirit. The soul is known and often described as the mirror world, the world that the inner traveler must enter to realize true evolution. In effect, one is synthesized through the soul where it establishes contact with the divine or heavenly spirit. The divine spirit is present in each of us; it is the self, the genius, the "I." Therefore, in a way it is "on earth as it is in heaven." It is also "as below, so above" and "as above, so below."

The soul is connected with the unconscious, the instincts and the animal nature that serves our earthly experiences. The soul represents the feminine, passive, negative nature and desires satisfaction. In the unevolved soul, satisfaction is a result of the fulfillment of the sensual desires that are those of the earthly body. Our lower nature is experienced through the unevolved soul, the senses.

In the evolving human being, there is a struggle for higher values. The soul is awakened through the activity and communication with the divine spirit, the self. It is through this action that we expand consciousness and become adept at constructively directing our instinctual nature. We struggle with our souls, our unconscious, to find balance between the spiritual and material worlds. We know that the goal of the physical body, the satisfaction of the senses, and the goal of the spirit, higher values, must be balanced through the soul. So it is not exactly "on earth as it is in heaven," as man on earth faces conflict with the environment.

The spirit is connected with the will, the masculine, active nature. The spirit is the higher octave of the ego. It is our conscious, our selves, and the light. The spirit moves us. The process of evolution is based on the spirit realizing the soul. It is based on the conscious shining light on the unconscious.

When the spirit is not directing the unconscious, it is perceived as the personal ego. The soul is realized by the spirit so that they do not harm each other and so that they may work together for the mutual benefit of each of us. The spirit, soul, and physical body are separate entities manifesting as a common effect.

The spirit may be visualized as the king, the soul as the queen, and the physical body as the servant.

As the human being evolves, the soul becomes transparent, enlightened, and purified. A cleansing of the soul occurs, and the light of consciousness beams forth. The strength of the spirit is manifested in the will, and this will guides and fortifies the soul.

The soul is inorganic, and the spirit is organic. The soul is uplifted and given life when the heavenly spirit realizes it. It is magic that gives life to the inorganic, and there are no words that can begin to express it. It is metamorphosis. The soul is the cocoon of the spirit.

2. Balance

It is through spiritual evolution that we harmonize with nature and reach the heights of ecstasy, love, and oneness with all. Each of us searches for higher values, and in this search we are pushed from one extreme to another in order to reach a balance and conform to nature. During this struggle, we begin to realize our own nature and how it affects every part of our beings. And if we keep working at this, we come to know our own nature and we come to know God, who is within us. The microcosm—in this case, man—becomes part of the macrocosm, nature. It is through this harmony that we as evolutionary beings achieve satisfaction and inner peace.

On earth, we struggle to balance the needs of our spirits, souls, and physical bodies. And through our souls, which are continuously agitated, we strive to rise above our lower animal desires. By finding this balance within ourselves and controlling our desires, we come into contact with our higher selves, the spirit. It is this struggle that leads us to the knowledge of free will and predestination.

On one hand, our indomitable wills can be exerted against the environment. It is through this battle with the elements that we discover our advantages and disadvantages in our personal approach to life. We realize that this arduous struggle is not "my will, but thine." It is at this point that we realize and gain confidence that this struggle and our fates are a dual responsibility. It is true that "thy will be done," but human beings, possessing inborn intelligence, have the propensity for developing foresight and thereby enlightening their futures through the experience of the past. Using free will and foresight, we assure for ourselves a secure and fruitful destiny. We free ourselves from anxiety and gain inner peace. Each of us at the core of our beings wants to develop ourselves and to upgrade our destinies. It is through the strength of our wills, our spirits, that we satisfy the needs of body and soul. It seems

3

that in this struggle we undergo suffering, but we should not suffer too much or have too much pleasure. Life is somewhere in the middle. It is a balance.

Nature has many cycles, of which all living things are a part. Birth, life, and death belong to nature, and man strives to understand the many cycles of nature. The beginning of the cycle followed by the end unceasingly gives way to a new beginning. In the physical world, we beacon heart and mind not to be sad when life ends.

Spiritual evolution is a continuous struggle from two extremes toward the center.

Spirit, Soul, Physical Body

At first, we struggle against our own natures. We struggle to realign that part of ourselves that has evoked conflict and disharmony within us. Then we struggle in the opposite direction so that our own inner natures come into harmony with nature. This process is called polarization. We polarize our intelligence with wisdom, our emotions with love, and through the soul, our physical bodies with the spirit. We attract and we are attracted and through this process we become centered. At this center, we achieve balance. We create an inner wheel that generates power through our whole beings. It is at the center that we find an electromagnetic field where there is unity of masculine and feminine, spirit and soul. We all possess masculine and feminine elements within ourselves. Out of nothing comes everything. It is the activity of the spirit, the will, that reveals the beauty and strength of the individual. In addition to the forcefulness of human nature, we see that we possess inner fortitude. Activity is grace. Struggle is evolution.

3. Activity

It is activity that consummates life, and there is activity in everything upon the earth. In life, no one is chosen. Evolution and the power of nature operate through us all. When we are in harmony with nature, we reduce our hardships and enhance the quality of our life. We love life and respect nature. We are like a healthy organ of the body that functions for the good of the whole. We are not special, as we are not more important than other vital organs. We may be specialized, however, as our duties are different from those of our fellow men and women.

When we act in opposition to nature or are completely passive, allowing nature to act upon us arbitrarily, we experience disharmony. Either we punish ourselves or life punishes us. Each human being is responsible to his or her human duties, and we are predetermined only toward evolution.

Harmony with nature is possible through our sensitivity. Evolution is not a thinking process but rather a feeling process. It is synthesis rather than analysis. Feeling has the mysterious ability to give dimension to the intellect. Feeling takes the dryness of intellect and humidifies it. It gives compassion and mercifulness to mankind and takes away the pitilessness. The heart, mind, and spirit combine to make the human being its rare and creative self.

When we think too much, the mind can grow weary and ache with no relief. The brain can feel like a stomach that has been overindulged. The mind becomes exhausted and resistant until it seems combustible. The intellect explodes. There is no clarity, only confusion. There is no vision.

It is the vision, the image, the imagination that is created from feelings and sensitivity. The human being doesn't want to suffer and simultaneously feels the need to suffer. It is this catharsis that elicits and brings forth the human spirit. It is a smoldering inner fire that is purified by the fire of the divine spirit. The fire below purifies to become the fire above. The intellect then grows to understand what is beyond it. We need only get a glimpse of our higher natures to recognize our earthliness and that it is indeed our lower natures. Our lower natures are not apparent to us until the divine being within has awakened us. It is the same if a person does not know good from evil. There is no direction where there is a lack of conscience. There are morally insane people who are not in contact with the divine spirit, God.

We approach life unconsciously. Slowly, through the process of evolution, encompassing the struggle for higher values, we advance and unfold into consciousness. Traveling and assisting the path of spiritual evolution is a tremendous advantage for the outer life as well as the inner life. As stated previously, we evolve from two directions at once. We evolve from the inner values and the outer values to the center, where we find our human equilibrium, life. We don't withdraw from society and head for the woods. We stand alone and apart from the false values of society to develop our inner resources. We then draw upon those inner resources to develop a meaningful lifestyle for ourselves. We set a good example for our fellow men. We knit together our kindred spirit with others. It is through visualizing those dreams that please the heart and the mind that we reach out to embrace others. It is through our friendships with others that we approach our goals and create a virtual force. A virtual force is created from the meshing of the spirit, be it in the church, in sport, or in the nation. It's the collective support, the momentum that you get when you intertwine the spirit in each man to form one energy, one spirit, God.

Life is a series of births, deaths, and transformations. It happens on all levels: intellectually, emotionally, and eventually physically. The cycles of nature are endless. For the student of life it is an ongoing adventure of hidden and symbolic treasure. You may die to fear and be born to be courageous. You may struggle with your emotions and intellect and then turn from the cold, egotistical side of life to the warm, compassionate style of the humanitarian.

When we transform our own natures to nature and God, we advance our spiritual evolution. When we integrate the echelons of ourselves, we become powerful and interdependent. The one who is patient and dedicated is in touch with the divine spirit within. We are in harmony with nature and operate through it. We function together and in harmony with kindred spirits.

4. Time & Space

Spiritual evolution, spirit, soul, rebirth, and God are very beautiful words. But words have no dimension. Works have dimension. Time and space give dimension and understanding to our thoughts, words, and deeds. Time and space are axioms of life upon which hinge understanding.

Suffering is the element of time and space. Suffering gives a purpose. It gives life to life. Because life is lived mostly on an unconscious level, suffering activates the thinking and feeling processes and expands human consciousness. Suffering is not an aim but a need. With thinking only, we would be robots. But it is imagination, suffering, and our tolerance for sweating it out that clearly differentiates us from the computer. It is the human soul and its suffering that render man superior. It is the divine spirit that gives life to the inorganic and to the soul. It is suffering that forces the spirit to rise like the phoenix. The spirit is the real and invincible self. It is the spirit that uplifts us.

Suffering makes a person evolve and grow. It has an internal pull like a vacuum that sucks you inside of yourself. Unexpectedly, everything external to the self becomes valueless. Surviving and dealing with physical or emotional pain awaken the inner being. Suffering draws the human being into the inescapable moment. It is the moment of darkness and loneliness. Suffering cleanses the soul and enlivens it. Through suffering, we evolve to know God, the divine spirit within us.

Transformation is the key to spiritual evolution, and it is suffering that serves as the vehicle of transformation. Transformation or suffering are not motivating factors in themselves. It is through the illusory, fantastic, and imaginative whole of our beings that we envision a purpose that motivates and brings about transformation. It is our struggle toward realizing our illusions that creates a confrontation with reality. The illusion is shattered through the element of time and space. It is an end that is to be followed by a new beginning.

Through this process, we strengthen our wills and are more determined toward our goals. Through suffering, we draw nearer to bringing forth our good fortune and happiness. Our life sufferings are synthesized into the motivating force of our realities. In the search for ourselves, we begin to detect the more subtle differences between the sensual and spiritual. The sensual world is highly subjective, and the spiritual world is the clear vision of reality. It is in the physical and emotional suffering through our senses that the divine spirit is born. The spirit doesn't know suffering. It is free in consciousness. We suffer when we are locked in our unconscious, our souls, and cannot escape our senses. In time and space, through evolution, transformation, and suffering, we are something made from nothing. We are the Alpha and Omega. We are the spark brought forth from divinity.

House 2: Aquarius

Masculine, Fixed, Air

5. Character

So long as we are on earth, suffering is necessary for evolution. But as I mentioned earlier, life is not meant to be too much suffering or too much pleasure. It is a balance. It is possible to improve upon the quality of suffering. Suffering can be constructive. We can weave it like a fine golden thread through our characters. We can give design and form to suffering. Artistically manifested, suffering can resolve our fear and apprehension about the future. We can begin to use suffering as a passageway and a stimulus for foresight and preparation. We transcend the problems of anxiety and suffering through foresight and preparation. We achieve inner peace.

We have a choice between upgrading and downgrading our destinies. We have a choice between honest and neurotic suffering. When a human being suffers honestly, he begins by accepting life and finding a purpose in it. When we suffer in a neurotic way, we deny life. By trying to avoid suffering, we complicate it.

The human being is good and bad, masculine and feminine, active and passive, electric and magnetic. Mankind is a rare concoction of conflicting ingredients. The recipe is unique for each of us. A little of this and a little of that make us the unique beings that we are. Naturally, there are many influences that manifest themselves through our characters. There are also factors such as genetics, diet, environment, education, destiny, and free will. There are countless influences that compose the complete individual. All of these influences blended together reveal the values of a person. The archetype in astrology teaches us that character is destiny.

10

We suffer when we are imbalanced. We suffer from extremes of either too much or too little. When individuals have a philosophy, they learn to suffer honestly. They play the game of life and are optimistic, cheerful, and glad for each day. They are strong, and they get something out of life. They anticipate obstacles and conflicts with the environment and they learn to take it. They persevere in the face of setbacks and disappointments. They are not aggressive and willful in the quest to achieve their goals. They do not harm others, and if they can help, they are delighted to do so. They are the good citizens. They have a goal along with a plan for achieving it. "When you achieve something in the right way, it will be a source of happiness and will be maintained." What is truly yours cannot be taken away. This knowledge and wisdom becomes a human duty. It is best accomplished by setting a good example.

We suffer to achieve our goals. It takes time and patience to realize a goal. It takes intellect and wisdom. There is a saying, "Go slowly and you will arrive sooner." Life is an active experience that builds the foundation for the attainment of our highest ideals. Honest suffering is not so bad and it is necessary for achieving goals and continuing spiritual growth. Anxiety is a form of suffering and for a short time may act as a catalyst to activating our goals. Anxiety drives us to seek inner peace. When anxiety pushes you toward this inner goal, it may be considered positive. When anxiety develops into fear, however, it is a paralysis and it prevents us from moving ahead. Anxiety is having too much foresight and is generally considered negative and neurotic.

Neurotic suffering complicates our lives and compounds our illusions when we are greatly attracted or attached to the desires that are perceived by the senses. Those of us who cannot master self-discipline are unable to attain happiness. We will get less out of life if we are not willing to give to life. When we run against time and space and try to accelerate in time or when we are always playing it safe, we can become stagnant and not achieve inner peace. When our needs conflict with our ethics, we will never know the virtue of accomplishment. Those who use the bicycle method to get ahead, to push another down while they push themselves up, will be the source of their own unhappiness. When we cannot let go or become too detached, we harm others and we harm ourselves. There is no difference between self-destruction and auto-destruction. It is an imbalance. "What is achieved in the wrong way will be a source of unhappiness and will be lost." Some human beings suffer from severe anxiety, insanity, disease, and isolation. These are the people who wanted to avoid suffering and gain complete freedom. Suffering is the mechanism of evolution. We should learn how to suffer.

It is difficult to maintain sensitivity and ethics; nevertheless, we should maintain this ideal. The best we can do is to set a good example and harbor no hatred, envy, or false pride for our courageous sufferings. We should learn to defend our human dignity and our future.

6. Good & Evil

Good and evil can be brought out in all of us. It isn't so difficult to understand that under random circumstances we have a propensity toward evil as well as good. The world is filled with good apples and bad apples, but this isn't an indication that all the apples will turn bad. The individual does not have to be suffocated under the hand of destiny. If man activates his free will through a struggle with his emotions and intellect, he will obtain the right thinking and develop the right instincts. Eventually he will be transformed into an evolving being who possesses a refinement of nature that will motivate him to help upgrade human destiny. Humanity, in general, is afflicted with social problems. But more and more, the outsiders have a greater chance of seizing happiness. It is certain that good and dedicated people will have to suffer for their ideals until the bad ones are touched by understanding and shown an alternative. A good human being is balanced between good and evil. Our purpose shouldn't be to judge but rather to have compassion and set a good example for others to follow.

The illusions of life unfurl and are shattered one by one until the human spirit is revealed. When our illusions are shattered, it causes us to suffer. When things are not the way we think they are, we are disillusioned. It is painful to experience delusion, but it's more painful to hang on desperately to illusion.

Mankind seems to have a need to suffer, and when we don't know patience, foresight, intelligence, and wisdom, we seek neurotic solutions. By our own natures, we attract and are attracted to situations that reinforce our insecurities. When we can't see clearly and are confused, we become pessimistic and melancholic. Pessimism spoils the mind. Neurotic suffering is a placebo. It accommodates our need to suffer without the satisfaction of achieving our goals.

Suffering is beautiful when it is awakening, directed, and meaningful. It is positive when through it we arrive at our goals. Through suffering we become compassionate. *Ecce homo.*

7. Development

Good fortune comes to those who work toward it. It is through suffering that man ripens and becomes an individual. It is through the struggle for higher values, goals and understanding that we fulfill our deepest needs. It is the fulfillment of these recessed needs of our unconscious that life culminates in happiness. It is the search for individual purpose that motivates us. Each of us needs to find a niche in life. When we become useful and purposeful, it spurs us on to greater longevity. So have what the French call a *raison d'etre,* a reason to be. We must attempt to succeed in the relationships of life. We must try to satisfy our unknown selves so that we may attain our inner peace. We extend our personal selves into society, thus becoming the microcosm within the macrocosm. We associate with other members of society who have a likeness to ourselves. "Tell me with whom you go, and I'll tell you who you are." We take on a collective identity. We qualify for the true society when we assume responsibility for ourselves and our functions in society. We realize our potentials as well as our limitations. We become a link in society.

The events of life are linked together in a chain-like pattern. Each individual is a responsible and independent link in the chain. As a functioning part of the chain, we cannot break away nor rely on the strength of any other link. Our spirits are connected in a similar way, and each of us tries to connect ourselves in a way that assures solidarity. We don't take on the burden of any other link but our own, and by managing our own parts we reinforce the total strength and garner our own individual source of power. It is the responsibility of each link to realize its inner and outer strength, to show a determination toward evolution and toward heaven and God. Spirits are linked together in silence and in the process there is divine guidance, which is communicated through each successive link to the end, which is the beginning.

14

Our problems are not solely our own, but rather they are social problems. They result from an inability to function collectively. When we cannot establish a framework from which to operate as a necessary component of life, our thinking becomes misguided. The wrong thinking ultimately affects us in a way that creates suffering for all of society.

We attain our hopes and wishes by having the right thinking. We attain them by becoming ethical and moral. Morality is a social standard and varies from society to society. Ethics have their roots in the laws of nature and they serve as our inner guides. Morality, however, is contained in ethics and both are our human duty. We are known for our accomplishments but seldom remembered. Ideally we are dedicated and relate to others through friendship. In this process of socialization, we learn to extend ourselves to others and to accept some obligation to them. We cultivate humanitarianism and grow closer to knowing love.

House 3: Capricorn

Feminine, Cardinal, Earth

8. Friendship & Love

The foundation of love is friendship. Love is built on friendship. A friendship offers its bonus—companionship—and on a higher level it offers a spiritual bond that acts as a wireless system of communication. Friendship is mutual support and reinforcement of our inner securities as well as our common triumphs over the environment. Friendship means to give to someone what he or she needs as differentiated from what he or she wants. We give neither too much nor too little.

We upgrade human destiny when we encourage and help our fellow man toward higher goals. We become unhappy when we try to escape from our obligations and when our aim at purposefulness is thwarted. We flee convention in an attempt to free ourselves from social pressures only to realize that total freedom doesn't exist. Total freedom is isolation and is no freedom at all.

Friendship is an obligation. Our friendship and love deepen through the development of our higher values. We become unhappy when we cannot maintain our independence and don't belong to ourselves. We are unhappy when we are not whole within ourselves. When we don't relate to others, we experience a kind of social disease that complicates our lives and makes them artificial. Human beings become slaves to society and great pretenders, making them unhappy when they are not surrounded at every moment by people who flatter them. They are vain. Under these circumstances man becomes superficial and tiring. We cannot get from others what we do not have in ourselves.

We advance in our evolution when we accept humanity without anger or resentment. If we resent others, they will not help us. Each one of us must learn to know ourselves. When we know ourselves, we will know others. Each one of us is a part of the self. When we know others, we will know ourselves.

Failure is manifested through the wrong thinking. To fail means to decide for something that we really do not want. Success is generated through the right thinking and reinforces our inner values. The human being is unique yet a part of the whole of mankind. We explore and discover the whole of our beings in others, who represent a part. When we feel anger toward another, it is important to question ourselves, and we will find that what angers us the most in others is in ourselves. We put it in the mirror. It is possible to retain our ideals, but as we mature, we become more realistic. The realist expects nothing from others while the idealist sets a good example. We learn to accept the human being as a human being, nothing more and nothing less.

Although we are unique, we are also the same. We desire love, friendship, spirituality, expansion, security, and communication. What is on the surface of man is not necessarily what is underneath. We need to look behind the mask to discover the real self. Our individuality lives through our distinctive ways of attainment and ultimately lives through our eternal spirits. Man is motivated by satisfaction in the discovery of himself. We are attracted to those who bring us nearer to our inner peace. It is important to make others feel secure and allow them human dignity.

9. Goals

It is necessary in life to have a goal. Just choose a direction and stay with it. We need to know what we want and how we are going to achieve it. Without this aim, we are already going backward. In approaching a goal, it is better to go slowly so that we can avoid as many mistakes as possible. Mistakes cost us time, and it is not good to waste time. Our goals should be like diamonds that are clear-cut with precision so as to expose their radiance. When we possess clarity of purpose, we can then assimilate every facet of ourselves to conform to nature. We establish a system that aids us in the accomplishment of our goals. We can become organized and determine exactly how much we can accomplish in the year. Time is a closed system that we can learn to use in an intelligent way. By using time intelligently, we can lessen our anxieties. We have an itinerary that guides us on our long journey. As we strive for inner peace and approach our goals, we collate learning experiences that contribute to our overall understanding of life.

Life must be approached on some level, and it is finding this level that is one of the most difficult problems. There is the humble approach and the exalted approach that represent the extremes. One extreme gives feelings of elation while the other produces depression. Naturally, the idea suggests finding the middle path and that is where we will find our inner peace. When we find the level, we begin to get a better grip on reality.

Life compels us and commits us and once we accept the obligation, there is no way out of it. Life entices us and then we are hooked. It is too late to turn back. There are no more branches off the road. There are no more illusions. You see your goal clearly. Sometimes we meet with obstacles that prevent us from moving forward. We are attracted to our goals and at the same time we are pushed away. Sometimes we have to struggle to control the inner resentment and maintain a certain detachment from our desires and those things to which we are attracted. This way we get perspective and find balance. Life is simple if you don't want anything from it. Life is learning to be your own friend.

There are many pitfalls in pursuing a goal. The darkness seems to come from outside. Darkness is born of fear, anxiety, and superstition. Light is born of inner peace. If we move ahead without foresight or are paralyzed by too much foresight, we encounter setbacks. It isn't easy to reach our goals when we are provoked by inner conflicts and encounter conflicts with the environment. It takes the delicate precision of a fine mind and spiritual values to attain happiness. It takes inner fortitude to stick to a goal. Preparation, independence, and the will to persevere lead us to our goal. It is in the evening of life that we face the lonely moment of truth in the finality of our accomplishments.

There is a Hungarian saying, "It is the happy minute that makes the happy hour; the happy hour, the happy day; the happy day, the happy year; the happy years, the happy life." What cannot be achieved in the hour cannot be achieved in the lifetime.

10. Work

We refer to our lives' work as a profession. Life itself is a kind of occupational therapy. We should love our work. A profession gives us a healthy way to work out our psychologies. It is through our lives' work that we achieve our hopes and wishes. We struggle for our professions by starting at the beginning and going step by step. Ideally, through a profession, we will realize financial security, be of service to humanity, and build a solid foundation for the future. When we approach our professions in this way, other people see that we have values.

What are values? This is a word that is terribly vague. It seems to take in all sorts of stray notions. Now even if we are able to communicate what we think are our values, it would be a greater task to observe those values that we have described. Values are very difficult to see clearly if we don't have a sharp frame of reference. In other words, to see a red rose on a pink background compared to a red rose on a red background. We learn to distinguish our values through our work.

It is ironic that the values that we think we are projecting are often not being interpreted as we imagine. Whenever I am curious about a person, I listen to him or her describe another person, and he or she is usually describing himself or herself. Therefore, it is an illusion to look for love, security, and admiration in others if we lack those things within ourselves. You cannot get from others what you don't have yourself. It is necessary to develop our inner beings and to find love and security in the depths of our own souls. It is the contents of our souls, our unconscious that reveals itself to others and yet remains a stranger to us. We are in search of our souls. We struggle toward a greater consciousness while conflict smolders in society. This turns the search for our souls into an inferno and a descent into hell. Man is the highest creation above the animal, the vegetable, and the inorganic material, yet man could learn much from these creations about the order of nature. We attempt to realize our unconscious, our souls, under very chaotic circumstances. Therefore, we must be truthful with ourselves so that we may advance toward evolution. We want to evolve.

Often the values that we set out to define go unseen by the receiver. What prevents the exteriorization of values is attachment. Passion, greed, and ego are blinding and require suspension of the self. To display our values to others, we must be independent in our emotions, secure, and have a sense of ourselves. Others may then begin to see us more clearly. When we respect ourselves, others will respect us.

It is the inner strength of an individual that gives the rest of mankind a peaceful reflection of their souls. By giving a good example, it encourages others to draw upon their inner resources. It encourages them to develop security, to give love, and to find positive reinforcement within the self. When we seek approval from others, we are unable to establish an authentic relationship of love and friendship, and that causes us to suffer. It is as if we are trying to measure our own self-worth through measuring the love that another has for us. We are trying to hang on to something that doesn't belong to us. Only what is within us belongs to us. A poor psychology can create a boomerang effect. Everything is cause and effect in action.

It is not easy to cut away the false values from the true values. The true values are not realized through the senses. The true values are known to every soul. The only thing that differentiates one human being from another is their values. Life has a value. Life is simple if you don't want anything from it.

House 4: Sagittarius

Masculine, Mutable, Fire

11. Self-Realization

It seems that the purpose of life is to realize the self. The realization of the self is a mystery that we seek to uncover. Every illusion must be shattered, and through these experiences we become our own truths. To find the self is a search that goes on life long. Through our experiences, we find many clues that lead ultimately to the unveiling of the real self. The real self cannot be destroyed. It is invincible and presides over the human body and the senses.

In this earthly incarnation, we seem to evolve through our personal suffering. We are alone in this world, and we are nothing to others. Man is a wolf to man. We should not despair at this aloneness. At the root of aloneness, there begins suffering and therein lies the hope of finding the self.

The self is the one remaining fragment of our dissolution that is left when everything in this earthly life has been abandoned or has abandoned us. The self is the core of the human being. It is the immortal spirit. The self is veiled in colorful images, grand fantasies, and illusion. Each experience in life is pursued to the end. The experience is the cycle within the cycle. An experience is born, and through the accumulation of these experiences more information is deducted. Each illusion and fantasy lives in reality or dies in delusion. All experiences serve the purpose of unveiling the self. They help us to assimilate our individual realities and give substance to them. The mystery of the self is synthesized through our life experiences.

All of us have been given intelligence. It is a tool that may be used constructively or destructively, and it is our free will to choose. We have a destiny to fulfill, and we have our free will to choose the higher or lower path. Given all of this, we will not fail to win at life. We will realize the divine self, the inner light, the spirit of man.

We are in a constant state of struggle. Through change, we keep reaching out to take in as much as possible so that we can expand and grow richer in experience. We struggle to realize our destinies, and it is in our characters that we find these seeds. Everything that we are, we also become. Our ethics and our morality find form in our future. There is no escaping our destinies. However, there is the potential for improvement. There is the potential for upgrading our destinies. Through struggle, we gain understanding of ourselves as well as others. Through struggle, we gain inner security and confidence in our futures. We can change our psychologies, thereby changing the trajectory of our futures. We struggle to see outside of ourselves. We can then see how we fit into the whole of mankind. We struggle to achieve the right thinking. The proof of right thinking is realized in cause and effect. The right thinking will yield the right results. The results are a source of happiness to us. Happiness and accomplishment act as catalysts. It is our satisfaction in having ethics and morals that motivate us. It is the realization of the self on the highest level of consciousness. It is the continuous search and struggle for that end that brings out the best in us. This process allows us to work off of others energies. Other people, especially friends, awaken our desires and stimulate our actions. Our actions are a result of our-selves and an expression of our individuality.

12. Past, Present & Future

It takes a strong will to endure the struggle toward evolution, and more than that, it takes a very refined nature to reach self-realization. Through this self-mastery we become aware of the subtle vibrations of the divine within us, our spirits. This life-long process could be called squaring the circle. It is the process of struggle that develops our inner most natures.

It is through our spiritual evolution that we bring forth our unconscious. The beauty of our own souls can never be realized if it is not brought out. If it is not brought out, it is not. It is impossible for the genius to be seen if we are afraid to suffer and struggle toward consciousness.

The past, present, and future coexist, and it has been said, "What was, is, and shall be." So in life, the spirit of man can be seen in the same way. Imagination is the seed of the unconscious and realization of the unconscious is its flower. It is birth, death, and rebirth. Imagination is the gold thread that sews together suffering and good fortune, uniting heaven and earth.

It is the will, the volition that makes all things possible. Nothing can be realized without the will. The will comes out as we realize our-selves and our unconscious. The will is the intangible difference between life and death. The will is the cause of the self. It is the driving force of the spirit. To know the self is the beginning of understanding everlasting life. It is the realization of God who is the life force, the self. It is life's gusher, and it is like tapping an oil well. Through our will to suffer, every layer is penetrated and the passageway is cleared so that the life force can be aspired. Life comes from the inside out. Life isn't reversible. Death comes from the outside in. Until man de-blocks the passageway of the life force, that which is outside will decay. The body will pass away. The self doesn't ever die, but it is impossible to realize eternal life until we have broadened consciousness. Firstly, the individual conscious must be realized and then the collective conscious. We enter the brotherhood of mankind with our spirits akin.

It is through time and space that all things come to pass. It is through loneliness and isolation that we find substance. It is something that comes from nothing. There is no past without the future and no future without the past. There is no time and no space, there is here and now. It is the moment of consciousness. We realize that the unevolved soul and the senses are what anchor us to the earth. The "will" to go away from earth and toward heaven is the genius, the individuality, and the self of man.

13. God

I have never had the impression that God is almighty, yet I stand in fear of God with whom I am one. God is in every living being and me. God is my higher self. God manifests in the heavenly spirit and that is what I am destined to realize. Also, I must confess that evil is also in every living being. Good and evil are ethics. Evil is on earth and it is mine to choose. My soul belongs to me. It is of the earth and senses but may also be realized by the divine spirit. My spirit belongs to God. It is divine and comes from heaven above. The human being is a winged beast that doesn't want to fly. We are body, soul, and spirit. We are intelligence, emotion, and love. We are superior to the angel and superior to the serpent. We are metaphysical.

God is everywhere: in the air we breathe, in the food we eat, in the water we drink. God is animate and inanimate, organic and inorganic. God is alive. God is music, art, dance, and love. God is one. God is two. God is three. God is nowhere and everywhere. God speaks through our mouths, hears through our ears, feels through our hearts, and thinks through our minds. Sometimes we are not good listeners. We hear the wrong words. We are sometimes confused and walk to the beat of a different drummer. We are human beings and sometimes make mistakes. We are very wonderful. Each of us is a part of God. God manifests through nature and evolution. As each human being realizes his or her true self, his or her divine spirit unites in consciousness. That person's spirit unites with the spirit of other human beings, and that forms one energy, one force, one God. God is infinity. God is nature. God is awareness.

So we also have hell. And hell is the fragmentation of consciousness. When we are in disharmony, we create hell on earth. It is hatred that exists between people and between nations. It is suffering of the most pitiless kind. It is endless pain, and it is vanity. Hell is the eviction of the divine being within us. Look through God's eyes and see the beauty of human nature and listen through His ears and hear the rhythm. I have always wondered how one could convey all the marvelous and touching wisdom that is in nature. Where would one begin? How could one communicate its hidden beauty?

14. Truth

Since life is a cycle, it seems that you can begin at any point. What truths are communicated is universal. No matter what point in the cycle that you begin, you can apply the knowledge to yourself. Where it begins is where it ends, and where it ends is where it begins. You can examine the full cycle of nature. Much of our communication is complicated by the interpretation of the one receiving information and the one telling it.

There are three ways in which something is communicated. They are the way it is said, the way it is meant, and the way it is heard. The one receiving information colors the truth and so does the one communicating it. Our truths lie hidden in obscurity. When we hear something, we should receive it on three levels: that of the spirit, the soul, and the physical body. It is quite certain that we hear what we want to hear and see only what we want to see. This applies to all of the senses.

Many people don't communicate at all. You hear words that say one thing but underneath you get a different message. When the superficiality wears away, there is something else beneath the surface. A person can instinctively tell if another has respect for him. There are many underlying springs of knowledge that can be synthesized through consciousness. We gain knowledge through helping other people, and we give knowledge to help others. The consciousness bursts forth without direction or it blooms forth in creativity. We have the possibility for having well-ordered instincts or rather a well-ordered unconscious. Through knowledge and communication we find the dividing line between the unconscious and the conscious or the instincts and the volition. We can look out into this world through the eye of the senses or through the eye of God, which finds the highest level of communication beyond the senses, which is called clairvoyance and clairaudience. It is the inner vision and the inner voice.

Wisdom is every raindrop; it is everywhere in nature. Everywhere in nature there is beauty and harmony to be found. There is a season to everything. In our lives, there are the spring, summer, fall, and winter. Each season is a time in each of our lives for a purpose. We should try to stay in harmony with the season that is of our age groups. In spring, we are planting; in summer, we are cultivating; in the fall, we harvest; and in the winter, we benefit from our efforts.

Life is a giant network of communication. When we desire and have the courage to know the signposts of nature, everything is revealed to us. We open the eyes and ears of our inner beings, and we speak through our inner voices.

House 5: Scorpio

Feminine, Fixed, Water

15. Power

Who in the world has power? The one who chases it yet it eludes him in every possible way. The one who does everything that is humanly possible to obtain what belongs solely to nature. Some people try to contain power as if it is something that we can possess. This kind of power is non-dimensional. It is impotent. Power cannot be owned or contained by anyone. The only opportunity for us to possess power is to open ourselves to the finer vibrations of nature and let these vibrations operate through us. We then work for the most powerful of creators, God. It is then, as much is humanly possible, that we become powerful beings. We have the magic of the universe at our fingertips. Every door is open to us, and we rise to a very advanced psychology in which we are able to guide the destiny of our fellow human beings. It is this bond between man and God that constitutes the brotherhood and sisterhood of mankind. It is the spiritual meeting place between heaven and earth. Power pursues the individual who knows from where he comes and to where he goes. When we master our own natures, we rule our own destinies. And when we rule our own destinies, it has many effects on the world. There are many effects from a cause and many causes for an effect. The powerful human being wields the power of good and evil, as these are both channels from which we realize our divine natures. We become powerful instruments of God. No one is a mastermind, but each of us possesses our own genius. Each human being's genius linked together with others makes the mastermind. We are each a piece of the puzzle that fit together to form the whole picture.

Life is very generous. When we know our genius, and we have our inner peace, then we are balanced. Our needs will always be provided for. We operate as part of one continuous flowing reservoir of love, will, and nature.

When we are unbalanced, the power of nature threatens us. We are crushed within the very machinery of our operations. When our inner order is disturbed, it makes us alien to everything in our environments. When life gives us an advantage, it also gives us a disadvantage. We should train ourselves to use both.

16. Imagination

Where did time, space, and infinity come from? Where has nature come from? Where and who is God? What was, is, and shall be. There is nothing new under the sun, except imagination. It is imagination that foretells the future. It is the genius to put things together in a way that realizes the future. The question isn't where is time, space, or God but rather can you imagine them. For God and nature have been, are, and will be. They are all.

There comes a moment in time when one faces the results of his or her work. The work is complete, and there is nothing further to do. Like a skillful scientist, you await the outcome of your hypothesis. You realize your theory through exacting visualization. You realize your dream.

It is very difficult to feel successful unless you have a goal in mind. You must make an effort to achieve success. You must plan your work and work your plan. It doesn't matter what your goal is as long as you have one. Next you need determination or will to get to your goal. It takes courage to step into darkness and feel your way around. It takes knowledge and wisdom to realize your goal. It takes silence. It takes love to find God and nature. There is French saying, "A little knowledge takes man away from God, a lot of knowledge brings him back again." In life, we must question everything, including our own goals and our thinking. We should stand before our goals and question their reality. We should reeducate ourselves so that our behavior conforms to reality. Reality is the vividness of our imagination, our vision. Our greatest truth is our love for our fellow man, and this is what lies at the core of our natures. It is this occult truth that we must see.

Our dreams are brought alive by being in harmony with nature. We become synchronized in time and space. This gives definition to our earthly existence and to our environment. Majesty is God given to each of us. Each of us is a tenant in the cycle of evolution, and through struggle and suffering we escalate to higher knowledge. Our dreams depend upon our careful cooperation with nature, God, the divine spirit. This is the higher path of human evolution.

To know God is an outlet that balances our inner and outer worlds. The soul of man acts as a matrix for the spirit. The soul is the womb from which the spirit aspires. There is a God. There is a plan. But there are no words.

17. Transformation

The comprehensive life process can be engaged only after we have attained higher knowledge. Through higher knowledge, we grow in understanding of the cycles of nature, God, the divine spirit. We discover the church in us. Man struggles to understand death. We find the level of our beings where we can integrate life and death. We visualize the middle ground, the gray area.

Given the activities of will, daring, and silence, we will find knowledge. Knowledge is a combination of both intellect and wisdom. We thirst for this knowledge that is hidden from us. We persevere in unearthing the mysteries of life. It is transformation that is attained through the evolutionary drive. It is the will that induces this drive.

Satisfaction is derived from the transformation of sexual energy into creative consciousness. It is the transformation of the soul that brings forth the subtle essence of life. The spirit enriches the soul. It is through our souls, our intuition, that we find the common bond that links life to death and death to life.

To understand the mysterious life process, we should initially look to the individual. By observing the simplicity of human beings, which are the microcosm, we can synthesize, identify, and understand life's master plan, the macrocosm.

Our conscious and unconscious are not what they appear to be. They are reversed like the mirror image. Our conscious is within. It is our inner beings, our selves, and our spirits. The conscious is the inner kingdom of the human being. The conscious is always growing, expanding, and is multidimensional. It operates on many levels and must realize the unconscious, the soul.

The conscious and unconscious, the spirit and the soul, seem to be aware of each other. They are the day and the night. The conscious exists with freedom from time and space. It is infinite. The unconscious is encapsulated in time and space. Life is for the most part still unconscious. It is through suffering that transformation occurs and shatters the illusions of the unconscious. Illusions become delusions. Suffering evokes awareness that broadens consciousness. Slowly, the conscious becomes aware of the needs of the unconscious. Consciousness exposes the self that is disguised by the mask of the unconscious.

The conscious directs the unconscious. The spirit satisfies the soul. It completes it and makes the human being whole. We become aware of our mystique. Consciousness is like a dam that when released generates great power. Release is accelerated through transformation. Consciousness is the star within our souls that connects us to the heavenly constellations. We are metaphysical.

18. Vision

Through knowing God, we develop our sixth sense that is connected with the pineal gland. We develop clairvoyance and clairaudience. Our sufferings become crystals. Our confusion changes into clear vision and clear listening. We express ourselves on three levels: the soul, the spirit, and the physical body. We integrate these three levels to create the whole human being. We shouldn't overlook the importance of the soul. That is where the spirit and body unite. The soul is our center. It is our home.

The problems of life lie in the search itself. It is here that suffering begins. Questioning life is the fuel that suffering loves. We learn to take suffering. We learn to have compassion and give truth in small doses. In life, we pay for everything. We pay for what we want, and we pay for what we don't want.

There is good and bad in everything. They are opposite. When you see one, you also see the other. No one is pure in his or her nature. We are all good and bad. There are degrees. When you do too much good, you are doing harm. Life is a balance.

The unconscious, our soul, reflects our innermost needs. It is our core. We cannot deceive the unconscious. The conscious must realize the unconscious in order to upgrade our destinies.

The conscious, our spirits, is the energy source of our beings. It is like the sun that is a power source to the earth. The conscious, sun, is how we see ourselves. The soul eclipses the spirit. We cannot truly experience our own existences. We are strangers to the psychological world that exists outside of ourselves. We deceive ourselves often as a way of protecting the unconscious. It is our secret. It is a sort of hyperbole that affects our inner selves. It is a miracle to be understood.

In the conscious, we try to get an understanding of the unforeseen. "Foresight is the mother of wisdom." The unconscious is quite different from the conscious. The conscious is a dupe of the image, a refraction of the unconscious. Much control can be gained over the unconscious. Through the right thinking, we can develop well-ordered instincts. The conscious then has the power to save the human intellect. It is the ghostwriter. The conscious is unavailable to us in the logical sense, yet it inspires the whole of mankind toward evolution. It is a mysterious and unlikely equation that cannot be solved by deductive or inductive reasoning, but rather only by analogy. By drawing parallels, we can begin to make sense out of a complicated system. It is difficult from the mere point of presentation.

We are in search of our souls, our unconscious. The soul is a mirror. It is the unknown contents of ourselves that we see reflected in others. Life is an orchestration of human souls and their ascension to the divine spirit. The spirit is the light in our souls.

House 6: Libra

Masculine, Cardinal, Air

19. Cycles

We think of the cycles of life. In the Bible "there is time for every purpose under heaven." We should think on death. Death is frightening, yet it is really the fear of fear—the fear that time will escape us. We rush back and forth between the past and the future without being in the present. It is most difficult to position ourselves in the present. But one method would be to become an observer. We can learn to be vigilant about everything that is going on around us. We can develop awareness. There is time for everything in the present. Doing and being is the art of the present. Doing separates life from death. We should belong to the past, present, and future. There is no future without the past and no past without the future.

Whatever is, was, and shall be. Time and space solve all problems. Patience is the only virtue. The past, present, and future coexist. So in our lives we can deduct the future from the past. All change takes place in the present. The present changes through our knowledge and learning from past experience. By changing the present, we change the future.

We fear death and this reaches to the very root of our human problems. We fear failure and we fear success. What is beyond failure? What is beyond success? What is beyond death? All of us will die. Death is in the nature of things. Aging, sickness, putrefaction are stages leading to death. We fear that no one will remember us. But to fear death is already in the future and it negates life in the present. Life is now: in the day, in the moment, in the breath of the spirit.

It is necessary to consider the past because it is in the past that we find our destinies. It is by understanding and examining the past that we see where things need to be changed. Also we must look ahead briefly to the end of our lives before we are able to judge the quality of our lives. We must judge the evening before the day has past. We find hope when we use foresight. We learn foresight through experience. Good and bad is inherent in all experiences. There is no life without death, no success without failure, and no love without hate. It is in the destiny of every human being. Death will always be a subtle anxiety as long as we live.

Death is a troublesome subject. It seems so final. It reminds us that we are alone. To live life fully, we must become comfortable with the idea of death. We need to integrate life with death. We realize that life is a cycle, and death is a part of nature. We can learn to live life with the peacefulness of death. Nature has arranged for death to be like most things. It is the opposite of what you think. Dying will be easy because you don't think that you are alone and dying, you think that the world is coming to an end.

There will be another beginning, reincarnation, or rebirth. It is that way in all of nature.

20. Death

Death exists only in the unconscious where our existence is transitory. Death exists until we become more advanced in our evolution. It is the attainment of complete consciousness that shatters the illusion of death.

It is possible to avoid cataclysmic physical and emotional suffering by self-discipline, patience, love, and conforming to nature. We can align our natures and realize that our purpose is to serve humanity.

We have a choice between the higher self and the lower self. The unconscious choice is that of acceptance, and the conscious choice is to apply knowledge and wisdom. Knowledge suggests that we are responsible for our actions.

The ancients believed that the first physical cause was located in The First Heaven (Primum Mobile), the first mover. Therefore, the cause of life, nature, God, and their evidence in all things are visualized through our imaginations.

The past is the springboard to the future. It is the beginning and the end. What is past is now and in the future. It is the past that needs careful scrutinizing. It is in the present that we can apply wisdom and knowledge that is the seed of the future. The seed alone is love. Love is the cause of life. It is the fruit that we bear. Love is the messenger.

21. Relationships

Relationships have always had a storybook romantic appeal that has been imbedded deep in the psyche. Sometimes it isn't clear, but then the same theme emerges again and again. When I find myself in an impossible situation, I imagine Prince Charming coming to my rescue. This of course is an illusion. Prince Charming is an actor. He is a shadow. It is difficult to face reality when you have underlying conflicts: one tape with unconscious recorded needs and the other tape trying to satisfy conscious needs. This is a tangled web.

A relationship is a friendship, and your partner is only a human being. He or she is like you in that he or she wants many of the same basic things. You cannot approach your partner head on, but you must go through the axis of friendship and love. We need relationships for communication. We need others to reflect upon ourselves. We need warmth, kindness, and companionship. We need others so that we can polarize ourselves with them. Through our relationships with others we are becoming centered individuals. We become balanced and in harmony.

Women and men seem to be alienated from each other. This has led to the destruction of the family structure. We need to redevelop the foundation for cooperation between men and women. We should try to be more honest with each other, more yielding, and at liberty with each other.

We have suffered many delusions and this has left us feeling very thin-skinned and vulnerable. We are reticent about new beginnings or commitments to our future together. We are so sensitive to ourselves that we forget to be sensitive to others. Friendship is the key to a fulfilling relationship. It reflects our self-respect. It communicates what our soul desires. A relationship is completion.

22. Marriage

Marriage is a funny institution in that those who are in want out and those who are out want in. We have passed through an era where many people were against marriage. In fact, they were demolishing it. Basically, we need to give some order to a relationship and marriage is practical. It is the basis of the family unit. It requires us to realign our thinking and reorganize our internal affairs. This is the time to set new goals for the relationship. It is a time to broaden and expand an institution that has previously been unsatisfactory at our current stage of evolution. This means to experience the joys of a personal friendship. It means to work together and independently for the betterment of our future. Each of us can contribute in our special way. Traditionally, men put women on pedestals so that they could know if it was safe to go ahead. The pedestal has toppled, and it is time to travel the road to achievement in mutual support and friendship and as equals.

The old mold of marriage has been broken. The ingredients that go into a successful marriage have their inception in friendship. The physical and emotional have left us longing for spiritual growth. We desire compassion, companionship, consideration, and cooperation.

Basically, you marry yourself. You don't need to be fearful or have anxiety connected with marriage. You can't make a mistake in choosing a marriage partner because you marry yourself. You can't get divorced until you get married. People are good or bad depending on what we bring out in them. A good marriage is consideration and it isn't ideal. It has its highs and lows. Most importantly, be kind to your partner because no one is perfect.

From marriage and the roots established through the making of a home, we reinforce our sense of security. We create a constructive and protective environment for our children, who are the future of mankind.

Marriage also has to do with ethics. It is a commitment. It is ethical to conform to the morals of the society in which we live. Marriage is a contract. Marriage and the family unit are a part of the whole of our country. It is the heart of the world. The home, the family, and the neighborhood are the building blocks of the city, the nation, and the world.

House 7: Virgo

Feminine, Mutable, Earth

23. Instincts

Our instincts are responsible for the survival of the human race. But sometimes our instincts are beguiling. We are in the process of becoming more conscious, and it is consciousness that is needed for our continued life on earth. It is organization that creates a foundation for happy living. Everyone needs roots, a family, and a home. It is this need that simplifies a complicated world.

Women play a very important role and should be aware of the responsibility that they possess with regard to our destiny. Women should grow in the understanding of their role. Everything is synthesized through the feminine, earth mother, and she should not dominate but rather provide an atmosphere of support and reinforcement for her family. We learn that to seize love, we must let go of it.

Women can help man in his release from bondage by reflecting his feminine soul. She can make it possible for him to integrate the masculine and feminine within himself. Otherwise, he is always trying to suppress his own feminine nature. Masculine and feminine is in each of us, male and female. Man is receptive as well as aggressive. It is aggression that has created war. It is the polarization of masculine and feminine that will bring forth man's love and further man's understanding beyond his instinct for survival.

The instinct for reproduction is a feminine quality and is born by the woman. It is her instincts that must link us with others. A marriage, for example, is dependent upon the woman for its survival just as life is dependent on the feminine nature for its survival.

The world awaits the woman who is not the shadow of a man but knows her own nature and reveals it. When we show our own natures, we are more likely to find someone who is like ourselves. A woman is the counterpart of a man, his soul reflector. She is the half, and together they are the whole. He is the king and she is the queen. It is the feminine nature that is the primal force of the universe, and it is she that must deliver mankind to its evolution. Women should reveal the strength that lies in their femininity, negativity, and receptivity. They possess the power to attract.

It is women's subservience to what they perceive as security that denies a man the knowledge of his own love. We fail to attract man toward his evolution. Should women remain sublime? Or should they gravitate toward aggression and masculinity? Mankind is faced with the possibility of involution. Women should reach out to men as the mother reaches out to the child. That is the beauty of femininity. But reach only halfway, as a man has to reach halfway also. There is an order in everything; therefore, let men and women work together joyfully. We shouldn't seek to be important in the world but we should find a purpose for our lives. We must strive together to provide a family unit.

Men, women, and children can be satisfied when there is order.

24. Polarization

Marriage in the metaphysical sense is the unity of heart and mind, soul and spirit. It takes all of these qualities to ensure the right choices in life. To choose the right partner, you have to search for the person who has the same values that you do. You have to choose someone who has the same ethics and morals. By choosing the right partner, you can grow and evolve together. You marry yourself. The ability to bring out the best in others rests with each of us. If the effect is bad, we need to examine ourselves more closely to determine the cause. Each of us is a cause and an effect. We realize who we are through our relationships with others.

In many cultures, divorce is forbidden. Only in exceptional cases, such as the inability or the refusal of the woman to have a child or desertion, have been grounds for divorce. Even serious physical disabilities have not been grounds for divorce. In most cases, divorce is self-denial.

Ideally, men and women should polarize through their relationships, and their children should complement their relationship. Everyone who we meet is an opportunity for us to balance ourselves.

People are the richest source of information and can circulate it quite efficiently. It is possible to bring out the spirituality in each of us and join the chain of clan destiny. What we like most in others is ourselves. In a marriage, both partners should struggle to balance themselves and this will make their marriage a good one. Better is the enemy of good.

25. Health

Good health begins by choosing healthy parents. Since we had no control over this, we are left to do the best that we can for ourselves. Robust health is contingent upon the practice of good health habits. Each of us is entitled to good health, especially when good habits are developed at an early age and minimal damage has been incurred. Good health, a strong constitution, and good vitality depend on a well-balanced diet, fresh drinking water, adequate exercise, proper elimination, and a good psychology. Good health results from self-discipline. It is the self-discipline to stay away from excesses in food and drink. It is the self-discipline to choose and stick to a routine of diet and exercise. Walking is an excellent form of exercise and can easily fit into the day without preparation. It has many benefits, such as regulating breathing, breathing air deeply into the lungs, and clearing the mind of anxiety. Naturally, a healthy psychology builds a healthy body.

It is difficult to determine whether a disease originates from a psychological or a physical cause. Certainly a bad psychology is wearing to the body and leaves it vulnerable to bacterial invasion. Over long periods of time, a bad psychology may manifest itself in any variety of maladies ranging from asthma to cancer. There is medicine for sicknesses, and holistic medicine is taking aim at the cause rather than the effect that is traditionally the concern of allopathic medicine.

Sometimes sickness can be an escape. The unconscious, without direction of the conscious, can manifest physical illness. Sickness may be perceived by the unconscious as a way of avoiding obligation and responsibility. Accidents may also be classified as an unconscious aim. It is through our own psychologies that we may circumvent ourselves. Serious accidents ending in paralysis or permanent damage to the physical body are sometimes unconscious responses to deeper psychological issues. It is paralysis manifested on the physical level. Accidents and sicknesses could be mitigated by the adjustment of our thinking and by changing our psychologies. We could evolve to a less violent future. There are no accidents in the universe. Nothing is random. Victims do not fail to meet those who will victimize them. The imbalance in our psychologies can make us actors with chosen parts. In some sense, we find a solution that is not satisfactory. Death, ultimately, is a blessing and a punishment. When we lose our will, we accelerate our own demise. We lose contact with the divine spirit in us.

House 8: Leo

Masculine, Fixed, Fire

26. Patience

It is the imbalance in human psychology that produces the extremes that are destructive to health and life. Since we are greatly responsible for our destinies, it should be in our power to live a long, healthy life. Each of us is entitled to it. Health is the dividend of serving humanity and the result of a good psychology and good body maintenance.

Sicknesses manifest themselves in many ways. They seem to surface when we have an imbalance in our natures. Sickness is an expression of downgrading on the physical and psychological levels. The physical body rebels when we are too much attracted to the lower needs of our animal nature at the expense of the needs of our higher nature—higher nature being morals, ethics, and values.

Our health is influenced by our early years and by our genes. The intoxication begins with our parents, both physically and psychologically. As problems develop psychologically, we may be unaware of different paths. We undergo illusions, and because life is for the most part still unconscious, we don't question ourselves enough. We happen along life's unconscious path until we are face to face with a serious problem such as illness. Then we mature a lot. We can then begin to make new considerations and to restructure our values.

Physical illness can be so debilitating that anything but the idea of recovery is impossible to cope with. From sickness that is an effect, we can then make deductions about the cause. Sickness is precipitated by some kind of negligence or wrong thinking. At least this is true in the adult. It is forgetting to take care of ourselves. We should respect people who take care of themselves. Sickness is the division of our souls. It is a result of the unconscious becoming so incorrigible that it can no longer be directed by the conscious. Sickness can be terribly frightening, and it is a serious setback. It impedes all of our work. Everything stops dead. At this moment we feel that we are alone. We need people, and we want everything around us to remind us of how precious life is. We want the only thing that makes a difference . . . love. Sickness demands patience like nothing else on earth. It takes courage and hope and a dream to hang on to. Time seems endless when you are sick. Time is the worst torture, and every minute is an eternity. The stress and anxiety swallow us. It is a bitter fight. It is unjustifiable suffering.

Sickness is in the psychology. It is sought unconsciously as a refuge from an overwhelming situation. It is an answer, but not a solution. When our illusions become delusions, we can't face it. It is too many delusions that bring us to the breaking point and sometimes they manifest themselves physically. It is when our hopes and wishes are not built on a solid foundation that we self-destruct. When we are afraid of life and suffer through neglect and wrong thinking, this is a bad psychology. A bad psychology expresses itself in some way and the most convenient and unconscious form of expression is via the body. We stop connecting the dots. We don't see that we are making ourselves vulnerable. A bad psychology goes against nature, and this is disharmonious and adverse to good health. Carelessness with regard to health comes out as sickness. When you run against time and space, you are going to run smack into obstacles. It is like swimming against the current. It is impossible to do for any length of time. It is imperceptibility that allows us to go against nature.

When we are in harmony with nature, it is possible to move mountains. It is a law of water dynamics to go with the flow. You don't need to scramble to avoid the obstacle; nature forces you up and over each rock or obstacle effortlessly. Naturally, to be successful, you've got to put some effort into it. This creates resistance, but that is the price we pay for success. We must work for it.

Sometimes upon reexamining our psychologies we can understand exactly what has precipitated an illness. The wrong thinking is often experienced as frustration and delay of the realization of our goals. The development of hostility and resentment toward others is experienced because we perceive them as holding us back in our accomplishments. Our passions rejected can be vented as hatred. Sickness comes from not seeing the truth and from not satisfying the real values. We need love.

27. Guidance

One of the first steps toward recovery from illness is giving up anger. Anger keeps us from being well and festers within us. It makes our hearts sore. Illness cannot be blamed on anyone, not even ourselves, as there are so many influences that go beyond our conscious control. It is helpful to be your own friend. Our psychologies are backlogged with burdensome material passed on through the generations. Many of our problems result from not understanding what is in the unconscious. The unconscious is a conflict of confusions. The unconscious needs to be reordered.

Patience is important in regaining our health. Patience is the only virtue. Patience builds our inner fortitude and helps us to rebuild our psychologies on solid ground. Patience softens us.

Love makes us well again. When we love, we are compassionate. Compassion is sympathetic to illness. Illness brings us closer to the divine spirit in us. It brings us nearer to God. There is a French saying, "A little knowledge takes us away from God, a lot of knowledge brings us back again." We can mitigate illness to some degree by serving those who are sick and suffering. We help others and upgrade our own destinies. We forgive.

It is other people who motivate us toward our work and accomplishments. It is other people who limit us and present obstacles. It takes an inordinate amount of faith to go ahead in the world with purpose and determination. It takes courage and hope and a constant reminder that we are each unique. We must believe that what we specialize in cannot be done by another. "Work and pray, pray and work."

As intelligent people, we find that to survive in the world requires the skill of reasoning. We send our ideas out upon the world and from this we receive feedback. We see the opposites and this helps us to understand the nature of things. Hot and cold, wet and dry, black and white, good and bad are all opposites. We should learn from the opposite. Nothing would exist if it weren't for opposites. There would be no boundary, no limitation, nothing with which to balance. Our souls are the same. They are limiting and confining. The soul is the vantage point. It is our playground. It is our turf. It is the point where man and God are synthesized. It is a semipermeable membrane. God is the higher concentration, and man is the lower concentration. It is osmosis. The soul is guided. It is the mirror. "The eyes are the mirror of the soul." Sickness and suffering are also seen in the eyes. The soul is the outer world, cold and wet. We are between the inner and outer worlds, and through our souls we commune with the divine spirit, God. It is the moment of darkness. But we evolve through the darkness to the light. The soul ties things together. The soul is the tie line to consciousness.

28. Love

Love is cheerful, warm, and demonstrative. Where there is love, there is the scent of sacred perfume. There is the prayer of the heart. Love comes from within us. Love gives without expectations; it is unconditional. Love fulfills every dream. Love motivates us. Love is the heart of our hearts. We are all of love and God. Love is our creation, it is our child. Love is like a waterfall, infinite and eternal. It is personal and spiritual. Love is like the sun; it warms and shines on all of life. But what can you do for the sun?

When you love someone, you love them on three levels. You love them on the physical, emotional, and intellectual level. It is being able to love on all levels that make us whole. When you withhold your love from someone on any level, you are withholding it from yourself.

Love isn't exclusive. It isn't jealous. Jealousy is inborn, but we struggle with ourselves so that we don't hurt another. We are all sensitive, but sensitivity means being sensitive to other people's feelings. Love and freedom don't go together. Freedom exists only in isolation. Love means to feel an obligation to another person. Need draws us closer to love. But we can't get love from anyone if we don't have it ourselves. Love emerges from our inner depths because we need other people. We have to become pliant to be accepted by others. Love frees us from loneliness, although we may be alone. Those who have love, give love.

When we love others it reflects our strength. It is a strength that comes to us when we really need it. Love is the gift of God and nature. Love is found everywhere and in everyone. People are good or bad depending on what we bring out in them. Love is the radiant energy of consciousness. Love inspires a good psychology. It makes us think and realize our mistakes. Without love, there is no life. Life without love would be fruitless and barren. Love changes us and awakens us. Love is the kingdom of God. Love is the hand of God. Love is full of hope. Love is our individuality. It is our perfect work. Love is a spiritual odyssey.

Love is the artist in our souls. Love is the phoenix rising from the ashes of death and destruction. Love is silence. Love is a dream. Love is real. When we have love, we can bear all things. We can take hatred, cruelty, and torture. We can take pain, sickness, and suffering. We can resolve the sins of mankind. Love heals and protects us. Love is a magi. Love is the mystery of life. Love is our hopes and wishes. Love is the pure heart that opens the doors to our inner worlds. Love is the child of sorrow. We are the children of God. When we love, we can let go. Love returns to love. Love is eternal.

House 9: Cancer

Feminine, Cardinal, Water

29. Ego

We shouldn't give too much because people don't want too much. Too much and too little are the enemies. To have inner peace we need to be balanced.

Probably nothing has ruined more dreams than our egos. The lower level of our consciousness is the ego. The ego is the biggest obstacle to our success and happiness. Its need for satisfaction is an enemy to our inner peace and to the achievement of our hopes and wishes. The ego should be monitored constantly so that it doesn't get out of hand and destroy everything. The ego can be modified by having a goal and by not reacting strongly to things. If one is fixated on a specific goal, the area in which the ego may become a threat is more easily detected. The accomplishment of the goal becomes the single most important thing and not the childish gratification of the ego. It is the absence of a goal that leads to a dilemma. We become self-consumed. Put your ego in your back pocket.

Sometimes we fail to be attracted to a goal. The unconscious is too powerful and enslaves us to our lower nature. Our ego takes over and we succeed at nothing. We can become desensitized and petty. We think that the world revolves around us and this delays our spiritual growth. We are all grains of sand.

When we strive upward toward the spirit, we progress toward our hopes and wishes. We attain satisfaction and tranquility. We rise above our egos and our senses long enough to perceive that there is a heaven above.

The ego is one of our greatest stumbling blocks. It provokes us to defend and attack when we are threatened. Our egos can become a heavy weight. Our egos fight without abandon and cost us dearly in time and confidence.

Our egos can make us think we are showing strength when in fact we are showing weakness. It is the reason we cannot take rejection. We walk away from things that we desire because our egos demand it. The ego, given the power, can make the satisfaction of itself a goal. It is the power drive.

We can use the power of our wills to tap into the higher level or our consciousness that is spiritual. The spirit is the self that never dies. It is immortal.

Love is our gift. Love realizes the soul and the needs of all human beings. Love is harmony. Love is on the inside. You have to search for love. You have to see through everything. Love is in the soul and the spirit. Love is in the eyes. Love is in the scent. Love is in the timbre of the voice. First, you have to find love in yourself. You should expect nothing. You cannot be given what you do not have.

In life, a bad person can never hurt a good person. A good person cannot help a bad person except by example. If in the end something good happens, it usually comes from your-self.

30. Self-knowledge

In order to understand ourselves, we must look at our psychologies. It is within the psyche that we possess a program. All the details of our lives are filed therein. Our experiences are filed with all relative information. It is the retrieval system that is responsible for memory, without which there would be no intelligence. It is the memory that causes us to suffer.

When we were children and in a less conscious state, we were unable to discriminate. We were like sponges, just absorbing information and emotions. It is this program that is responsible for our behavior. It is the basis of our reactions. For every action is a reaction. Reaction is a feminine quality. Action is a masculine quality. In our psychologies we find things that may need modification.

As we mature and come into more direct contact with other people and the environment, we realize which part of our psychologies is positive and which part is negative. When we are not moving forward toward our goals, it is because of a conflict. We can't achieve our goals, so we begin to examine our psychologies. We can be torn between two ideas that can't cooperate. A conflict arises when we can't make a decision and stick to it. A conflict is a blockage between the conscious and unconscious. The blockage can be removed by identifying the information in the unconscious that is acting as a barrier. Modern psychology examines these experiences in order to discover and disentangle the old program material. People go to psychologists and psychiatrists to be de-blocked. There is a solution to every problem. And as King Solomon said, "There is nothing new under the sun."

A conflict will eventually give way to excessive anxiety and that will motivate us to seek a solution. In a way, it is the misuse of intelligence that leads to neurotic anxiety.

Through reprogramming of our unconscious it is possible to attain the inner peace necessary to achieve our dreams.

A bad psychology comes from interferences. The bad psychology of the parents compounded through the generations. A bad psychology stems from having false values. Our values are the only difference between us. This reprogramming of the unconscious requires the use of consciousness. It depends on our ability to win against ourselves. We cannot be pure as in nature until we develop our psychologies. We cannot build a future until we understand the past. We marry for the purpose of forming a unit. Together as a couple we can fight the influences of the family. An undeveloped person blames his parents, an intelligent person blames himself, but a wise person blames no one.

It is possible to change our psychologies. The French say, "Change your nature." When we become tired of being in conflict with the environment, we search for a solution. It is self-discipline and the application of wisdom and intelligence that upgrades our destinies. It is all in the way we look at things. When we have a constructive psychology, we receive life in a different light. We give an illusion to life that is uplifting. We give to the experience an abstraction. We can take the torture out of time and space. We can give beauty and understanding to suffering. We can give elegance and continuity to change. Our happiness is our own responsibility. There is a lot of destruction going on in the world, but we are also destructive to ourselves. Life is in our hands; it is how we imagine it to be.

31. Psychology

Psychology can be categorized according to quality and quantity. For example, the psychology of a murderer is the same as that of a butcher or a surgeon. The psychology of a beggar is the same as a clergyman. The psychology of a thief is the same as a lawyer. The psychology of a businessman is the same as a psychopath. It is through upbringing, education, environment, and other influences that our psychologies are realized on different levels. The psychology of a murderer is carried out through different means. Some kill with a knife and some kill with a word. There is no difference except in degree. The ruthlessness can come out in the psychology. We kill for the soul and not for the body. If we love, we don't kill. Love can be brought out in someone more easily than hate. With guidance, we can work out our psychologies through our professions. We should love our work, and it should be therapeutic. With a good psychology, we can be helpful to other people. We are the cause of our psychologies and we are the effect of it.

Instincts are needed for survival. They are like the skin is to the physical body, a protective covering. The skin separates the inner from the outer. It detects heat and cold that signal the brain. The instincts in the same way alert us to possible danger. Sometimes, however, our instincts deceive us. We are not in control of the situation, but rather we are controlled by the situation. When we allow ourselves to be divinely guided and listen to our inner voices, we are protected.

Sometimes we come under the wrong influences. We are poisoned by our dissatisfaction with ourselves. The unconscious is in charge of our roots and needs, and we must make strides in getting those things or pay for these shortcomings. We must evolve, and the more the conscious is awakened, the less wear and tear on us. In this way the conscious realizes the unconscious. Our instincts are valuable to us when they are well ordered through consciousness.

When we don't have good instincts, we may not get the results we wish for. We may deceive ourselves. We have to work for greater awareness of the unconscious. Naturally, the instinct for survival will be maintained, but to make a decision based on instincts is risky business. Our instincts can be deceived and deceiving. The best idea is to think, to understand, and to use foresight. We should look ahead to the end.

House 10: Gemini

Masculine, Mutable, Air

32. Aging

It is the end of life that is again like the beginning. The elderly are in an unconscious state just as they have been as children. Instead of life coming into focus, it is fading away to some degree. The light of our once vital lives is becoming dimmer. But we can stay bright into old age as long as we are active in life. According to the book, *Raja Yoga or Mental Development*, by Yogi Ramacharaka, by giving attention to things, we are better able to remember. We can live full, long lives. But aging is part of the cycle of life. In nature, living things return to the ground. "Ashes to ashes, dust to dust."

It seems that as we age we should become more carefree. It is the winter when all of life's responsibilities should not be such a burden. It should be a time of great freedom and independence, which hasn't been possible until this time. It should be an active time, and it is a time when the need to be useful is critical.

It is difficult to imagine and define the time that leads to the final moment. It may be when the heart stops, breathing stops, and the vital signs are gone. At that point the body ceases to function. But we go on to eternity. Possibly we reincarnate so that we may come back and fulfill our evolutionary purposes.

Aging can be beneficial and filled with advantages that were denied to us in our youth. We can let go of anxieties and enjoy each moment of our lives. We can be healthy and useful and live lives of dignity. In order to have our dignity, we must have our will. The will to live is a great life force, and we must work life long to achieve our will.

We are the only links between heaven and earth and between God and matter. Maturity prepares us to leave behind our vehicle of this life on earth, the body. The spirit lives on in eternity, and we leave behind the children of our spirits, those who have His will in them.

33. Thinking

Thinking has excelled in importance over the years. Every piece of information that is taken in must be thought about to some degree. Thinking is the messenger. It is the system of communication that telegraphs information between the mind and the physical body. Thinking collects and coordinates messages from all the senses. Thinking is analysis.

Intelligence is important to spiritual evolution as it spawns our independence. We must think to become independent. When we are disciplined, we develop a well-organized system to discriminate incoming information. This accelerates our capacities for learning. It speeds up our thinking process and aids us in the expedition of decision making. Thinking is full of ideas and theories. Thinking is exact and precise. Thinking is the sharp edge of the knife. It is the ability to cut away information this is not valuable.

Thinking is important to the healthy psychology. Thinking allows us to organize and rationalize experiences. This allows us to avoid conflicts later on because of our attachment to consciousness. It can be packed neatly away in our memories.

Thinking should be combined with wisdom. When we use wisdom along with thinking, we begin to understand. When we understand, we are using more than thinking to interpret the information received through our senses. To understand, we must also let our hearts and souls be influenced. It is when we understand that we gain insight into ourselves and others, and we are at peace with ourselves. We are no longer suppressing unprocessed information that builds up and poisons our psychologies. Our understanding neutralizes a lot of hostility. It cuts out a lot of hurt. One of our worst enemies is the tongue. It is not kind to speak badly about another person. It shows that we don't know ourselves. "Know thyself and you will know the others." We should cut out the negativity so that we don't suffer the repercussions.

Suffering causes us to think and question life. It is intelligent to ask questions, however, the answer is contained in the question. It is wise to question ourselves first. The answers are within us. We can answer our own questions. We may not always want to see them, but the solutions are there for each of us.

The thinking process should be preceded by careful listening. You have to hear someone before you can understand. It doesn't mean just to listen to the words a person is saying, but to hear and interpret through all of your senses what a person means beneath his or her words. There are no words. Understanding comes through touching the soul of another person. It means that you can feel that person. People who listen have many friends.

Benjamin Disraeli said, "Man is not the creature of circumstances. Circumstances are the creatures of men."

34. Communication

Communication is vastly influential. The world depends on communication. The most personalized form of communication is word of mouth. Communication starts with the individual. When confusion and misunderstanding occur, we are not seeing things as they really are. Thinking is a tool that helps isolate and develop building blocks. By using these building blocks we gain independence. We should listen to our inner voices. When we acquire the self-discipline to think and listen, we are guided. "When the student is ready, the teacher appears." There is guidance for each of us. When we decide to think and to hear, we can do many things. Thinking is an activity that helps us to upgrade our destinies. We are capable of mitigating many circumstances.

Life is simple. We should learn to make decisions. It is courageous to make a decision and stick to it. It is better to decide than to be forced by indecision into a tight corner. It is better to try to achieve what you want than to be indifferent and accept what you don't want. We should take a chance on our dreams. We should plan how we are going to accomplish our goals. We should have an aim and make the best decisions we can.

We can combine our hearts and our souls with our thinking and become wise. We can synthesize. We should understand that there is more to life than the right answer. We realize that to see clearly, we must put the matter in the right light. We can see life differently by changing our own perspectives. The mind has a tendency to reverse images, and as a result we communicate in an upside-down manner. The mind seems to be the mirror image of the soul. By entering the mirror world, we learn to detect the difference between illusion and reality. By thinking, we interfere with the unconscious. By understanding, we become conscious. As long as we are locked in our unconscious, we don't move toward our spiritual evolutions. We drift aimlessly through life and fall victim to our self-created misery.

House 11: Taurus

Feminine, Fixed, Earth

35. Right and Wrong

The wrong thinking is the cause of our problems. The wrong choices and the wrong considerations destroy our health and our minds. The wrong thinking wastes our time. To waste time is the worst thing that we can do. We have to function as a whole in order to sift through and synthesize the mounds of information that comes before us. We should listen carefully to our inner voices so that we don't become confused. Mankind struggles to see and hear truth in a world that is always changing. It changes in time and space. Other factors are taken into consideration and the whole scope of life changes. When we take the right things into consideration, we have a different focus. Right and wrong are opposites. One cannot exist without the other. You have to see the opposites and then balance them. When we make the right choices, we begin to see the grand scheme of things. We can see the polarities. The truth is the way we see it. Man's thinking is right when he sees that there is good and bad in everything. We see that in some sense they are the same. We understand that for every advantage there is a disadvantage. We know that in life we pay for everything. We pay for what we want, and we pay for what we don't want. We learn through experience not to delude ourselves. We accept responsibility for ourselves, and we blame no one. We realize that by using free will, we can influence our destinies. We can escape the influences of the earth and of the sky. When we work with our God, we become powerful. When we are in harmony with nature, we are the masters of ourselves.

As human beings we should learn to concentrate. We should learn to use our minds effectively. Thinking should become a habit. Intelligence is inborn. Whether or not we use intelligence is our option. By using intelligence and wisdom, we are able to find solutions that give us satisfaction. Satisfaction is what motivates us.

We need to communicate. It is through helping others that we broaden and increase our intelligence. When we help others, they share their experiences with us. People are the most valuable source of information. It is through others that we find solutions. Life is a network of communication and an interchange of information. Life is repetition. Knowledge is valuable when it is applied to ourselves.

36. Satisfaction

It is through perfecting our thinking that we establish satisfying goals. So many people have cited their main goal to be the making of money. They have made money their God. It is necessary, of course, to be compensated monetarily for our efforts. Money is not the root of all evil, greed is. When we love our work, money comes very naturally to us. In life, when we are making an effort, our needs are taken care of. It is very important to love our work. Artists, actors, and dancers are fine examples of those who suffer for the love of their work. Only the best are remunerated. The key to their success is dedication. Dedication is an act of love. Money is not the motivating factor. Dedication comes from finding personal satisfaction in what you are doing. The real values are those that satisfy your soul. They are the values that give you inner peace.

The attraction to an environment that encourages us to adhere to our ethics and morality is preferable. Life is not ideal for spiritual evolution. We really have to create our own productive and spiritual environment. We shouldn't run away from life. Instead, we should stand up to it, and through our own example, one by one, the momentum begins to shift. The value of a single person is immeasurable. The action of one person can start a chain reaction. There are many effects from one cause and many causes for an effect.

37. Freedom

It is erroneous to believe that money buys freedom or happiness. Money buys illusions. Rich people can afford their illusions. Money buys necessities and it buys things of adornment for this life on earth. Money buys some of the things that we all wish for. Money does not buy freedom from suffering. More money means more obligations. We shouldn't make money our ultimate reward.

Finding satisfaction and inner peace in our lives is a reward. One of man's greatest challenges is to be useful and instrumental in guiding the destiny of mankind. We strive to make each day excellent and worthwhile. We should know what our goals are and have a plan to accomplish them. It is ideal to choose a profession that serves mankind and be compensated for it. Through serving mankind, we expand our intellectual horizons as we are all a tremendous source of knowledge. The ability to set goals and stick to them is imperative to a healthy psychology. Our discovery of our purpose in life is our *raison d'etre*.

We uproot our values in our search for love. It is finding a relationship of values that causes us to love. Higher values help us to find that which truly belongs to us. Whatever is truly ours cannot be taken away. Those things, such as health, love, and ethics, are ours to keep. No one can rob us of these things.

House 12: Aries

Masculine, Cardinal, Fire

38. Inner Peace

People need more than making money for the sake of making money. It is difficult to estimate how much money would make a person happy. It can only be said that we are never happy with less than what we are accustomed to. Young people are ambitious and want to be part of the world. They struggle with their ideas so that they can be successful in the world. They want positive reinforcement. Later in life, at about the age of forty, our values begin to change. We are experienced and approach life more thoughtfully. At forty, we begin to look for a more spiritual approach to life. By this time, we have fulfilled many of our obligations to our homes and families. We set out to apply the wisdom of our experiences. Our goals turn from the personal need to the needs of humanity as a whole. Theoretically, we approach life in keeping with those of our own age groups.

We should approach our goals with reverence. We should know exactly what we want and how we are going to accomplish it. It is this purposefulness that prevents us from departing from our goals. We should approach our goals slowly so that we make as few mistakes as possible and so that we don't harm others.

Money represents security to many people, but it is not really a hiding place. Money is a false value. Practically, we need money to survive. Therefore we should structure our lives on higher values. When life is approached in this way, it has a solid foundation. This doesn't mean that we should proselytize. We should always allow for the human dignity of the individual. It isn't helpful to push our values on someone else. Our own values serve others best by our example. No one wants to be with someone who is a truth serum.

Example is the best way of pointing something out in a nice way. We can never expect that someone will look at something differently when you argue. I believe that people would do better if they knew how. We should have patience and understanding with regard to our fellow men and women.

Need has a place in our lives. "There is a time to every purpose under heaven." Some of our most precious moments come from need. Need pushes us to create and to create is a need.

39. Humor

Life is a joke. Life is also serious. It takes real discrimination to know when to laugh and when to cry. You have to know what part of life to take to heart. You can't afford a broken heart.

The way you envision life is the way that it is. Your life is the way that you receive influences. Life is good and bad. Life is happiness and sorrow. It is all in the way you look at it. Life is in the eye of the beholder.

It is best to expect nothing. It is an advantage to belong to your-self. Everything seems to be against belonging to your-self, but you should be strong. People change very little in your own view of them. With understanding we accept the human being as a human being.

We can give to life a good or bad illusion. We can upgrade or downgrade our lives. We can create a masterpiece or produce a monster. It is a question of how we want to manage it. Life is life, and good and bad are a part of it. Good and bad are in the same container.

Sometimes things are not as they appear to be. The façade can be cheerful. It is nice to be cheerful and to play the game of life. Inside, it is heaven to know that there is indeed a purpose in our lives. It is reassuring to know that there is a God and there is a plan. It is a comfort to know that at the moment of your greatest aloneness you are not alone. In that split second you can feel the sweet touch of heaven around you. In that one moment of despair you can reach out to eternity. We are boundless with no subjectivity to time and space. We are emanating energy. We are not a body or a mind. We are not what we appear to be. The self is a force of infinity. The self is the philosophical black hole in a profound non-dimensional universe. Our selves are one with all. Our spirits know no anxiety or death. It is on earth that the self is incarnated. You take a body that serves you during this life.

The character of an individual is resembled in his or her physical appearance. The physical body is an expression of the inner self. The shape of the face, the eyes, the nose, the shape of the body, and the gestures are all a reflection of what goes on beneath the surface.

We can appreciate that everyone approaches life and its challenges in an assortment of ways. Some approach life theoretically, some impulsively, some emotionally, and others practically. We shouldn't assume that everyone sees life the way that we do.

Each of us is unique and has the potential for talent and genius. It is the genius in us that is the seed that is nourished so that it may be realized. Talent can be learned. It is the genius that comes from inside and therein lies the spectrum of individuality. It is the self that we are seeking.

Sometimes fragments of the self can be detected. They are like magnetic bubbles that are momentarily attracted into consciousness. There is scarcely time to examine them closely. But each time they appear, they can one by one be affixed and ordered in our unconscious. It is in consciousness that we bring forth unconscious material to be redesigned. The conscious realizes the external world of ideas and the intellect where we possess only the possibility for what already exists. We are much more than that. We are unique when from our inner selves we extract originality. We discover our inner purposes. Our meaningfulness comes from within.

40. Free Will

We win against ourselves when we succeed in revealing our unique selves. If we can discover the genius in ourselves, we leave our marks upon the world. The self is personal like a signature but much more so. It is I.

When we realize our selves, we also realize other people. We create a beautiful story by using our imagination and enjoying the beauty in our own natures. We take the routine of daily life in hand like an artist's brush and give beauty, grace, and simplicity to the details of life. We give illusion to life. We are like actors with scripts. A good actor brings the script to life. Life is the same. The individual must bring the world to life. Magic and miracles can only be seen through our own eyes. The magician gives an illusion. We should learn to create the magic in our lives. We can elevate our lives through spiritual qualities. Maybe at the end of life, we can put the magic kit away and our brief encounter with the world will be over. At the end, we can take our last bow for a fine performance.

To live without the will, the daring, the silence, and the knowledge to use magic would be a final regret. Life is a fantasy of our own making. The final obstacle is surmounted when we reach out to touch our dreams. Dreams do come true.

41. Mystery

Life is a mystery of love and God. Life is very simple. We have to let go of our lives to really understand it. We have to find the real security, which is the self. The self is immortal. The self is invincible. When we find ourselves, we will also find love and God. We will have evolved a lot. When we come to know this truth, we become powerful in our lives. We are the magicians, and no feat is impossible to us. We can grant the wishes of our fellow human beings. We can help others find happiness. We are happy when our deepest needs for love and God are satisfied. We are happy when we are of service to humanity. A magician is of help to others when they need him. He is in their dreams. Spiritual evolution means to realize the self. No one is chosen. We are one for all and all for one.

In each of us, we find the Father, Son, and Holy Ghost. We are the sons and daughters of God. God's spirit is in each of us. We are one with God and the divine spirit. We have everything within ourselves. We are an ingenious creation. We are the soul creations of the universe. We are full of faith. When we have done all that is in our power, it is our faith that delivers us to victory. Life is the love of God.

There is nothing to prove. When we give equally to the needs of our souls, our spiritual evolution and the needs of our senses, we are wise. We are going to do well in life. Everything in life is enriched when we go toward our higher natures. Dreams come alive when we think nice thoughts.